Eighty Days
and
Eighty Nights

Eighty Days
and
Eighty Nights

Wise Words for Everyday

Raymond Apple

iUniverse, Inc.
Bloomington

EIGHTY DAYS AND EIGHTY NIGHTS
Wise Words for Everyday

iUniverse books may be ordered through booksellers or by contacting:

iUniverse
1663 Liberty Drive
Bloomington, IN 47403
www.iuniverse.com
1-800-Authors (1-800-288-4677)

ISBN: 978-1-4759-4654-3 (sc)
ISBN: 978-1-4759-4655-0 (ebk)

Printed in the United States of America

iUniverse rev. date: 09/18/2012

Contents

Foreword...ix

1. Adulthood..1
2. Ambition...1
3. Anger 2
4. Beauty...2
5. Charity..3
6. Children..4
7. Compassion 5
8. Courage 5
9. Courtesy..6
10. Criticism 6
11. Death 7
12. Decisions...8
13. Doubt 9
14. Energy...9
15. Enthusiasm 10
16. Faith..11
17. Family 12
18. Fear 12
19. Food..13
20. Forgiveness 14
21. Freedom 14
22. Friendship 15
23. God..16
24. Goodness 16
25. Gratitude...17
26. Greatness...18
27. Guilt 18
28. Hands 19

29.   Happiness 19
30.   Health 20
31.   History 21
32.   Holiness 21
33.   Honesty 22
34.   Honour 23
35.   Hope 23
36.   Hospitality 24
37.   Humility 25
38.   Justice 25
39.   Language 26
40.   Laughter 27
41.   Leadership 27
42.   Leisure 28
43.   Life 28
44.   Light 29
45.   Loneliness 30
46.   Love 30
47.   Loyalty 31
48.   Man 32
49.   Miracles 32
50.   Money 33
51.   Night 33
52.   Old Age 34
53.   Peace 35
54.   Pleasure 35
55.   Popularity 36
56.   Power 37
57.   Praise 37
58.   Prayer 38
59.   Rain 39
60.   Reading 39
61.   Repentance 40
62.   Rules 41
63.   Sacrifice 41
64.   Silence 42
65.   Sin 43
66.   Song 43

67. Sorrow...44
68. Study..44
69. Sunshine 45
70. Superstition...46
71. Talk..46
72. Time 47
73. Tolerance...48
74. Travel 48
75. Trees...49
76. Truth..49
77. Wisdom 50
78. Work..51
79. Worry..51
80. Youth 52

About The Author...53

Foreword

King Solomon said that above all other things what he wanted was a wise heart (I Kings 3). In our generation we would probably re-phrase that as a wise *mind*, because we think wisdom is an intellectual quality that comes from the mind. The scholars certainly argue that "mind" is what is meant in Biblical psychology when the scriptural texts say "heart". Actually even if we take the word "heart" literally, King Solomon has a point. Wisdom is a combination of *thinking*—using the mind, and *feeling*—using the heart. The heart intuits the situation: the mind responds with a way ahead.

It is in that sense that this book is sub-titled "Wise Words for Everyday".

We live in a complex and sometimes frightening age and environment. If *our heart* is schooled in the arts of wise assessment, we feel acutely the difficult nature of the moment. If *our mind* is trained in the skills of wise responsiveness, we are able to look ahead and plan with a modicum of hope.

That's why the eighty themes that make up this book are approached in terms of challenge and response. Because the author is a religious leader, he constantly employs religious models of feeling and thinking. Because he is Jewish, he utilises material that is grounded in the Jewish tradition. Because his name—Raymond—is said to come from a Scandinavian source that means "wise counsellor", he dares to hope that he might have special means of contact with wise ideas.

It is flattering to know that a certain Freemason remarked to a friend not so long ago, "Rabbi Apple is the wisest man I ever met". It's a great compliment and I probably don't deserve it, but I pray that one day I might.

The title "Eighty Days and Eighty Nights" recalls Jules Verne with his "Eighty Days Around the World". This book is in no sense a travel guide, but it does point to themes that affect human beings in all parts of our world. Though we differ so greatly from one another, we all share the same existential anxieties and yearn for the same calmness and equanimity.

The Book of Job (Chapter 32) has a remarkable phrase, "The days will tell". Each one of the eighty days—and nights—in this book is designed to speak to every one of us. I hope my readers will have a listening ear—and that they will not only learn something from the eighty themes but enjoy the experience.

— RAYMOND APPLE

1. Adulthood

In "*As You Like It*", Act 2, Shakespeare painted a word picture of the staging posts in life. Everyone had their place, from the "muling and puking" infant to the "slipper'd pantaloon" . . . coming finally to second childhood, "sans teeth, sans eyes, sans everything". Long before, the Bible had a similar idea: "The child was a child" (implying, "the adult was an adult") and eventually one became a hoary head before whom others had to rise in respect. Now it seems everything has changed. Because of bracket-creep, little girl plays Mummy, and Mummy plays little girl. The ones who feel the most uncertain are the adults. They are no longer carefree children and have to display responsibility. They are not yet seniors and cannot say they're too tired. But by now they have—or should have—self-knowledge, energy and determination. They can do what only they can do, achieving immortality by reason of their deeds, and certainly by means of their descendants. Theirs is the hard stage of life, but it is where the victories are won. Hopefully there will be time to reflect later when the heat of battle is over. A rare prodigy will be an Alexander the Great, already winning kudos when young. A rare senior will be a Moses, driven and driving at 120. Yet the adult is more than just a bridge between childhood and old age. They are the ones who toil and build and achieve, without the awkwardness of youth or the tiredness of old age. God and history will judge them; their task is to give God and history something to assess.

2. Ambition

An Australian who overcame polio wrote a book called "I Can Jump Puddles!" An American educator interviewed at the age of 70 said he was still climbing mountains, at least metaphorically. In the Book of Genesis, Jacob dreams of a ladder that joins earth and heaven. Rabbinic sages put into God's mouth the words, "You have a ladder—so start climbing!" A moving film depicts a paralysed victim who determines, "I'm going to move that toe!" That's what ambition is, to jump puddles, to scale ladders and mountains, to move toes. The Ten Commandments tell you not to covet, but they don't tell you not to be ambitious. The Tenth Commandment needs to be looked at in full—it doesn't say,

"Don't desire a house!", but "Don't desire *your neighbour's* house!" It's fine to be impelled by desire in order to get somewhere, so long as it's not at someone else's expense. Choose your goals wisely and sensibly, and when you're almost at the goal, make sure there's another goal ahead. Always have a kettle on the boil. There will be obstacles, and you'll often need immense physical, mental and moral courage. You might never get to the moon, but you'll get further than you did in the past. You'll certainly get higher than those who never even try.

3. *Anger*

Anger is not such a bad thing. It shows that you feel deeply. Apathy and indifference are so much worse. Being cold or lukewarm can destroy your personality and allow evil to flourish. The Scriptural idiom for being angry literally means having *a quivering nose*. When something stirs you up and your nose quivers, you can't sit back and do nothing. But what should you do? Anger that turns into violence or intimidation is neither effective nor constructive. Anger that merely makes a noise doesn't change anything for the better. Anger you can't control is no cleansing storm, just a storm without any catharsis. The head of an organisation on whose board I served was a very efficient chairman and never lost his cool—except once. I said to him, "It's so out of character for you to lose your temper!" He replied, "Don't worry—I never lose my temper except on purpose!" Uncontrollable and uncontrolled anger is severely criticised by the ancient sages, who deem it a form of idolatry. One sage goes further and says, "Losing your temper leads to hell". Another says, "Anger and temper are death's executioners". All these comments deal with what anger does to you yourself. It lets off steam but doesn't necessarily improve anything. What is important is not just to be upset and show your feelings but to have ideas and options that can help to make things better.

4. *Beauty*

A family friend once congratulated my father on a certain job I had obtained. She said, "He didn't get it because of his good looks". I think she was paying me a compliment and saying it wasn't my appearance but my brains that won me the appointment. Good looks are not the best way into most jobs except in modelling, where different criteria apply. I am now much older and my doctor sometimes writes on my file, "Well appearing", I take that as a compliment too. It might mean that I look well; it might mean, "Not too bad looking for his age". I have never worried about my handsomeness or otherwise. I have never patronised one of the so-called temples of beauty. I have no interest in going to a beautician. My wife tells me I would think quite differently if I were a woman; I am sure she is right, as she is on many subjects. We find in the Bible that beauty was important to women as far back as we can investigate. Biblical literature speaks of love potions and cosmetic ointments. The ancient scholars were as male-chauvinist as they come, but they generally had beautiful wives. According to the Talmud, three things bring joy—a beautiful home, a beautiful wife and beautiful clothes. The Talmud also said that when you see a beautiful woman you should praise God who created beauty. Nonetheless, King Solomon said in the 31st chapter of Proverbs, "Beauty is vain and charm is fleeting; the woman who fears the Lord, she deserves praise". Looks are not as important as character, and character is even more important than brains.

5. *Charity*

It comes from a Latin root that means to love. From the same root we get the word "care". There are two aspects of charity—if you love you will care; if you care you will love. I am irked by telemarketers who perform their set speech about the most deserving charity in the world and how much I should donate. I don't mind giving, but I don't want anyone's hard sell. I would rather have the chance of developing a nice feeling for the organisation and genuinely wanting to help, which I always tried to do over the years when I sought people's financial support for this or that fund. I know it's a hard world and the funds can't pander to people like me, but in the long run it is my way that creates a climate of generosity. I know my religious codes tell me what percentage of my income to devote to charity, and I try to obey this obligation . . . but the same codes warn against giving too much. No-one should give away so much that they end up needing support themselves. An additional warning: charity is not only acts but attitudes. One shouldn't only give a donation or gift but also a smile, a kind word, a good thought. One of the greatest things you can do is to judge a person favourably. It is cheap and easy to criticise and only see a person's bad points. Charity of attitude means finding their good points and accentuating the positive. That's caring, that's loving.

6. Children

We live for a while in ourselves and forever in our children. The wise author of these words had a counterpart in an elderly man in an audience I addressed in London's East End. What he said, somewhat ungrammatically, was, "If we won't have no children, we won't have no future". All very well, but children are precious in themselves, not only because they provide our continuity. My wife and I looked at each of our babies and said, "What a beautiful miracle our child is!" We still think like this even though those children are now adults with children of their own. To bear a child is the supreme expression of creativity. To raise a child is the highest form of education. To abuse or abandon a child is the ultimate treachery. Children have to be able to run and dance and laugh and dream. To make this possible is the parent's privilege. It's not easy and never was. Hebrew has a phrase, *tza'ar giddul banim*, "the trouble of raising children". It often is a trouble—it squeezes out your innards, it exhausts your energy, it costs you money, it steals your sleep. There is a saying, "When they're little they don't let you sleep: when they're big they don't let you live". But did they ask you to let them be born? Did they consult you about how to lead them through the terrible twos and the other difficult moments of growth? But remember this: every child brings its own blessing into the world. Help the child along and you will see the blessing. Don't give up on your child. Don't become like King Herod who thought it would consolidate his power if he slew his children. Give the child every blessing you can, and you will help to make the child a blessing. You may not get any votes of thanks, but that isn't the point of the exercise.

7.   Compassion

"I feel for you"—that's what the English word compassion connotes. In the Latin original it has a particular nuance—*I suffer with you*. It's probably a feminine syndrome, since the Hebrew equivalent, *rachmanut*, is from *rechem*, a womb. If we stick with theology a moment more, Biblical vocabulary regards compassion as one of the attributes of the Almighty, and it insists that men as well as women have a religious and human duty to be compassionate to everyone, those who are chronic sufferers and others whose misery is acute and occasional. Sometimes the compassion which the occasion calls for is a cup of tea and some TLC. Sometimes it is a few dollars. A Quaker remarked, "Friend, my sympathy is worth a five pound note. How much is thine worth?" What is always good is to spare a friendly moment and extend a supportive arm. If anything acknowledges the personness of another human being, this is it. Martin Buber made a distinction between the "thou" and the "it". There are times to see the other as an "it" with whom we have a merely pragmatic and utilitarian association. There is also a time for a relationship with them as a "thou", with feelings, frailties and fears. What comes from the heart enters the heart.

8.   Courage

At Melbourne High School my school principal was Brigadier George Langley, a veteran of the two World Wars. We called him "The Brig" and quickly realised that his personality and opinions had been moulded and affected by his wartime experiences. No wonder his school assembly speeches often highlighted what he called "that lovely virtue—courage". Whether teenage boys really knew what he was talking about is debatable—but in my final year at the school, I for one discovered what he meant. My mother died, and I found myself having to face life as an adult. I won't say that the Brig was able to wave a magic wand to carry me through those final weeks of my school education. But I guess I found out that courage, the idea he prized so much, was bearing me up. Courage is the faith that the future will open up and envelop a person. It is the strength that derives from the Biblical assurance that underneath are the everlasting arms. It is the determination to keep going and rise above every day's challenges. It can be physical daring like the Greek heroes. It can be moral courage that impels you to do what others coldly suggest is illogical and uncalled for. Courage doesn't stop you crying, but it stops you giving way to despair. Arthur Koestler, whose views on many subjects I profoundly reject, rightly said, "Courage is never to let your actions be influenced by your fears".

9. Courtesy

In ancient Judea, Hillel and Shammai were intellectual rivals (maybe even real brothers) whom later generations misread. Hillel is pictured as gentle, polite and patient, and Shammai as irritable, rude and without human sympathy. The facts do not bear this out, especially since Shammai's principle was "Receive every person graciously". The commentators say that if one receives his fellow graciously, even though he has nothing to give him, he has given him the best gift in the world. "Receive every person graciously" clearly means being polite and courteous. This is the way in which my generation was brought up. We were taught manners—to greet people nicely, give them a kind word, thank them for hospitality, apologise if one couldn't do what they asked. Now it's a different world, and we are all the poorer. I know a certain person whose only response to a greeting is a grunt, but I am lucky that I even get that. When I saw a grandmother tell her grandson to stand up and give his seat in the bus to an old person, the child said, "Why?" The Bible said, "Stand up for the hoary head", but some children have never heard of the Bible. Courtesy is one of the four pillars of civilisation, all beginning with C—courtesy, consideration, conscience, and community. We all have our own list, whatever letter it begins with. It's all to the good because if the world rests on so many sets of pillars it will make life much more stable.

10. Criticism

Because I have a mind and conscience I can't always endorse what other people say. Fair enough, since they don't always endorse *my* views. The secret is to be fair (and polite) when you criticise. In the Greek myth, Psyche sorted out the seeds of good from the seeds of evil. We should all be Psyche, seeing the good as well as the evil in every situation or person and being careful in how we put it into words. By now you are used to me quoting the Bible so you won't mind the following quotation from Proverbs 3: "Whom the Lord loves, He chastises". God criticises, but out of love. A Yiddish writer, Mendele Mocher Sefarim, describes the women's wick-drawing circle which meets in one of the poverty-stricken houses of an old village. As the women make wicks they improvise prayers. "As we draw out this wick," they say, "may You think of our sainted grandfathers and grandmothers and let no pain or suffering come upon us; that the light of our husbands and children not be put out before their time, God forbid . . ." Mendele adds indignantly, "Laugh if you dare, and say it is all superstition and foolishness, but may there be many more such candles and many more such pious souls. Mock if you dare—and if you say that I am the biggest mocker of all, just know that when I criticise, I criticise out of love!"

11. *Death*

Is death an enemy or a friend? It can be either. Some people desperately want to stay alive, others desperately yearn to die. Death will come, but some want it to come much later and others hope for it much sooner. Death began after Adam and Eve's sin: God said, "When you eat the forbidden fruit, your eyes will be opened and you will die". Having your eyes opened is a metaphor for knowing you are mortal. Classical Christianity, however, had a different view. It said that because the first couple sinned, all human beings are morally tainted, and only if they accept belief in Jesus can there be salvation. Judaism does not accept the "moral taint" idea. It says that your fate depends on your deeds. You will die anyhow, but if you have lived a righteous life your soul will survive; otherwise it will be snuffed out like a candle. We don't know the details of life after death but we do know about life *before* death. A medieval author said: "Life joins together, death separates". Our concern should be the joining together, living with and for others, enriching the life of everyone we come across. Martin Buber says, "All real living is meeting"—another way of saying, "Life joins together".

There is so much to do on earth that we should all want to stay alive as long as possible. Thankfully medical science has enhanced our chances. It is a tragedy if someone feels, "Life no longer has anything for me. Let me die!" If necessary one may pray for an end to life, but one should not actively bring it about. Should one fear death? Dying we can fear, but apart from losing the joining together we should not fear being dead. Maybe it is spiritual ecstasy.

12. *Decisions*

"Do you want tea or coffee?" I know what the questioner means, but I still annoy them by saying "Yes". If my wife asks, "What shall we have for dinner?" I also tend to be difficult and answer simply, "You decide". There are innumerable versions of the marital dynamic of decision-making. An example: "I make the big decisions; my wife makes the small ones. I decide who'll be the next President of the United States; my wife decides whether to paint the house white or cream". Whoever you are, you are making decisions every day of your life. Hopefully you make up your own mind, using information, thinking and reason—and wisdom—in order to decide. Doing what your political party, your sports club, your rich relations, your next-door neighbour says, is to be a sheep that shuffles along with other sheep. One of the things that worries me is those who refuse to decide that there is (or isn't) a God, and take refuge in agnosticism, which in the end is merely a polite form of atheism. Bachya ibn Pakuda said, "Don't rely on If and Perhaps". If and Perhaps suggest that a person is too lazy to make up their mind. Sam Goldwyn remarked, "I'll give you a definite Maybe". When it comes to belief you know that you believe or you don't—and if you don't, why not have the courage to say so? It's also a worry when parents say they will give their child no religious commitment when young but let the child decide for him- or herself when they grow up. What a fantasy. If you give a child some religious experience whilst they are young and they later reject it, at least they know from the inside what it is that they don't believe in.

13. Doubt

Normally I agree with the logic of Maimonides. I can't, however, when it comes to attitudes to women, nor on the question of doubt. His view was, "May the Lord deliver us from doubt!" He would probably not like me quoting the New Testament, though he did say that one should accept the truth whatever its source, but his opinion of doubt seems to have a New Testament parallel in the 14th chapter of Romans which says, "He who doubts is damned". But a moment ago I was criticising agnosticism, and now I am defending doubt. Am I inconsistent? It all depends on what doubt means. The way I look at it, agnosticism is a refusal to make up one's mind. Doubt is the argument that there is or could be another point of view. At school and university I was trained in debating. The mark of a debater is the ability to take any side of an argument, sometimes without notice, and to convince the audience that it is right. Debating requires you to present your case convincingly and to rebut the opposition. The audience knows there are two sides to the coin. They hear one case and then the other, and they realise that neither is necessarily the last word. Points are awarded for each team's techniques of persuasion—but it's not merely technique that is involved but the right to doubt that either side has the entire truth. In life however it's more than a game. You *have* to decide one way or another, or maybe favour a third opinion that combines elements of the other two. Life is action, and you can't sit back and agnosticise. The one who is damned is not he who doubts but he that freezes his mind.

14. Energy

One of the nicest things anyone said about me was a comment by Moishe, a fellow student, "Apple has Shepherd's Bush legs". Of course it makes no sense without some context. We were residents at the theological seminary, Jews' College, in London's West End, and once in a while I walked (since orthodox Jews don't use transport on the Sabbath) to Shepherd's Bush Synagogue to chant the Scriptural reading. I didn't realise how fast I walked until I asked Moishe to come with me, hence the above comment. On Sabbaths I walked everywhere, even to Stamford Hill—a much longer distance—to visit my then fiancée. Whether I could do it these days I don't know. In any case Marian and I have been married for more than fifty years now, and the Bible says in Ecclesiastes Chapter 9, "Enjoy life with the wife you love". The same chapter says, "Whatsoever you find to do, do it with all your might". That is the Biblical view of doing things with energy, though a few verses further on it says, "Wisdom is better than strength". Putting the two passages together, we get the advice to do whatever you undertake with both energy and wisdom—a wonderful combination. I used to be a workaholic and could give seven speeches a day (during a three-day visit to Auckland, I gave 23 speeches!). My ministerial colleague Rev. Isidor Gluck told me what he had heard in Ireland, "If you want to work for nothing you'll never be idle!" It is true that a lot of the lecturing and counselling I did was extracurricular and my salaried job didn't require it all, so maybe I looked for work more than work looked for me. But this chapter is not about what I was or wasn't paid for but what advice I have about being energetic, and if my advice isn't clear yet, let me say it again—while you have energy, find ways to utilise it. But don't forget to combine the energy with some wisdom.

15. Enthusiasm

A colleague who couldn't say a "th" kept preaching about "entusiasm" and after a while everyone realised what he meant but they wondered why he didn't show more enthusiasm about correcting his linguistic deficiencies. Our seminary teacher of homiletics loved the saying (probably derived from Anon), "If you can't put fire in your sermon, put your sermon in the fire". The word "fire" occurs constantly in religion, probably deriving from the sacrifices that were burnt on the altar. Fire is an important religious metaphor: it stands for the warmth of spiritual emotion, the light of religious truth. Kierkegaard wrote in his essay, "Passion, Pleasure and Pain", "Other people may complain that the present age is wicked. I complain that it is wretched, because it lacks passion." It truly is a sign of wretchedness when a person cannot summon the passion to feel deeply about anything, especially about life itself. Moses was told in connection with the sacrificial ritual in the sanctuary, "Command Aaron . . ." and one commentator remarks,

"'Command' denotes 'With enthusiasm'". Whatever cause you have chosen to serve, work for it with energy—and enthusiasm. If you carry out a task perfunctorily, mechanically, in lack-lustre fashion, the cause will suffer, and your own soul will become deadened. Sir Walter Scott said, "Breathes there the man with soul so dead, who never to himself hath said, 'This is my own, my native land!'?" Maybe people don't get so worked up over their native land—a concomitant of emigration and exile—but one can pity the person whose soul has nothing at all to thrill about.

16. *Faith*

Reason works with the mind, faith with the soul. The mind sees the structure of the world and seeks an explanation for what it sees. The soul sees into reality and finds itself, in the words of the Hazon Ish, a sage of the 20th century, "moved and enraptured by the marvellous and insoluble riddle of the world". The soul does not find reason: it finds faith. Faith finds riddles and can live with them. Faith says with a person whose name we do not know, who scrawled on the wall of a cellar whilst hiding from the Nazis:

"I believe in the sun . . . even when it is not shining.

"I believe in love . . . even when I do not experience it.

"I believe in God . . . even when He is silent."

Faith says: There are more things in heaven and earth than the eye can behold. That which is not seen by the eye is visible to the soul. You can hear the "still small voice"—how eloquently it speaks! Not everything needs to be defined by physics and chemistry. Love for instance. I know love exists, even though—to use Talmudic phraseology—I cannot capture it in a fishing net. Can I be commanded to love someone? No, even though the Bible tells us to love God and our neighbour. If we know God, the love will follow. If we recognise the humanness of a neighbour, we can love them with all faults if any. What about faith? Classical Christianity promoted the proposition is that if you believe properly you have the way to salvation. I am not sure that is enough. Can faith be commanded? Surely it has to arise spontaneously. And if it doesn't, salvation is still possible. I prefer to think that you find your own salvation by means of your deeds. Ideally your faith will motivate your deeds—but even if it doesn't, the deeds are the test.

17. *Family*

A family begins with history. Its roots are in the blending of two individuals, sometimes from widely different traditions, who create a marriage community and expand it through children. Its personality is forged in shared experiences of mingled laughter and tears. Its solidarity emerges when its members feel at home and at ease with each other, able to be honest, open and trusting. Its resilience derives from the capacity to love and respect one another, even when you are of different generations, even when you disagree profoundly. Its moral force is created by its endeavour to stand for values as a yardstick for actions and attitudes. Its inspiration is born of its simultaneous commitment to the individual and the group. Beginning with history, it makes history, because it is dedicated to enriching the kaleidoscope of the future. If the family did not exist, it would have to be invented.

18. *Fear*

No-one is immune to fear. "I feel afraid" are three of the commonest words there are. "The Sound of Music" offers us an antidote: "Whenever I feel afraid, I hold my head erect". Keep your dignity, don't go to pieces, march ahead as if there weren't a problem—that's probably what the song means. It has been said that there's nothing to fear but fear. The Bible knew that kind of fear very well. It responded: you never fear alone: "Fear not," said God, "for I am with you". The Bible radically changed the question, however. It said, don't imagine that there is only one kind of fear, the fear that comes when you're frightened. That's the sort of fear that requires an effort of will to battle and overcome it. There's another kind of fear, however, which we should welcome and not try to erase. This fear Jacob felt at Beth El when he said (Genesis 28:17), "How awesome is this place!" The philosopher Abraham Joshua Heschel speaks of "amazed, wondering awe". The greatness of God, the majesty of the Creation, the grandeur of the human mind and heart—all are part of what the Bible calls the fear of God. It's not "I'm afraid of God" but "I am awed by Him". When I feel that kind of fear I am lifted out of myself and transported to a realm that is beyond the banal. There's nothing to fear other than not feeling that kind of fear.

19. Food

I once ran an adult course called "The Food Factor". I thought I would attract huge crowds but I had forgotten to organise free samples. Not that I was incapable of catering. I can cope in the kitchen except that I haven't yet learned to make cakes or biscuits. What I was trying to show was that you can characterise the culture of any people by its cuisine. Although my main focus was on Jewish cuisine I made the comment that Australia only became a really interesting place after mid-20th century immigration brought in so many culinary traditions. The same applies to the development of the arts. There were Australian music, art, dance and other cultural activities from the word go, including Aboriginal culture. But immigration brought an awakening, and Australia is now a vibrant society. Back to food: The proof of the pudding is in the eating, and eating deserves intellectual analysis. For its effect on physical health and psychological well-being, look at Psalm 104. Eating stimulates the mind and arouses the spirit. Food habits give the believer the feeling of serving God. There is a social aspect—eating together makes for community. I notice I haven't said a word about myself as an eater so let me add a final note that I long ago gave up meat. I don't denigrate the meat-eaters or try to convert them, but I find physical, psychological, spiritual and ethical value in living without meat. The story-book Jewish mother used to say, "*Ess, kinderlach, ess!*—Eat, darlings, eat!" She thought the way to be loved is through chicken soup. She would be aghast to think of chicken soup without the chicken.

20. *Forgiveness*

"Forgive and forget" is too glib a saying. It's often too hard to forget, but you can still forgive. An adage of the old rabbis was, "Don't judge your neighbour until you stand in his place". The author of this saying was Hillel, who knew that once you know what pressures a person faces you understand why he acts as he does. You don't have to endorse his actions, but you can forgive him. Freud said, "When I have forgiven a fellow everything, I am through with him". This doesn't mean that when you forgive a person you write them off. It means, "When I have forgiven him, the account is closed". That's what Voltaire may have been hinting when he said, "God will forgive—that's His job". Isaiah puts into the mouth of God the words, "I will blot out your transgression: I will not remember your sins." After forgiving us, He closes His account on that particular matter. Unfortunately we tend to restart transgressing and God has to forgive us all over again. His forgiveness may be boundless, but humans should not try Him too much. In the Apocrypha, Ben Sira warns (Chapter 5), "Add not sin to sin, counting on forgiveness." If you ask why we humans should forgive one another, one answer—based on "Love your neighbour as yourself" (Lev. 19)—might be, "Do unto others what you would wish them to do to you". Another—based on the same verse—is, "You are all part of each other: would you punish one hand for hurting the other?"

21. *Freedom*

Sir Asher Joel wrote a book called "Without Chains, Free". It was about the Philippines but it could have described the strivings of every people to be masters of their own destiny. The quintessential freedom struggle is the Hebrews as slaves to Pharaoh in Egypt. With their hands tied behind their back no nation ever had a chance to reach their full potential. What made it worse was that most people who lacked freedom not only had hands and feet that could not move freely, but their tongues could not speak, their minds could not think, their dignity was degraded. What a wonder that their spirits could still soar above their sufferings and their souls could still sing, albeit inwardly. What a pity that they were often so poorly served by their own leaders who so often committed crimes against their own people in the name of freedom and became tyrants and totalitarians themselves. A Biblical narrative tells of a rebellion led by Korah, Datan and Aviram. Their team at first includes On Ben Pelet, who then drops out of the story—according to legend, because his wife told him not to be a fool. "Whoever wins," she said, "you're still going to be a nobody, so get out while you still can!" Freedom is a precious thing. As justice must be pursued justly, so freedom must be sought strenuously but administered fairly.

22. Friendship

What is a friend? Someone with whom you are able—and allowed—to be yourself. Before a friend you don't put on airs. You don't pretend or act. A friend knows your quirks and foibles and doesn't give up on you. Neither of you is perfect. You are honest with each other, you quarrel, you disagree, you feel disappointed, you walk away, but you stick with each other. A friend understands you. Nothing can kill their trust and loyalty. Sometimes you are apart for years on end but when you meet up again the old spirit returns. That's what a friend is. A friend is there in time of trouble. A friend doesn't need to read you a sermon. A friend is just there. Yes, there are false friends, fair weather friends, friends who seem to drop you. Heinrich Heine lamented, "My friends and gnats together have gone with the sunny weather". You can do without the gnats, the flies, the mosquitoes. But if the friends evaporate with the end of summer, they weren't real friends at all. Sometimes you both feel bad about it and would love to find your way back. A social worker said in a lecture recently, "Buy some Danish pastries, go to their house at a time you know they'll be in, ring the doorbell and say, 'Here's morning tea. Put the kettle on—we have to talk.'" She is adamant that it works. You become a friend because friendship happens, not because you consciously decide on it. Solomon Ibn Gavirol said, "Let not a thousand friends seem too many in your eyes". I say, let not one friend seem too few.

23. *God*

Biblical Man knew he was in the Divine presence. Most people still pay lip service to God, whatever name they give Him, but not the secular humanists. They recognise traces of religion in the culture of the environment but they call them leftovers from the past. Let others have and/or practise a religious faith; they themselves can live without God and find their poetry elsewhere, and their ethics. Intellectually, emotionally, this is an untenable position. Louis Jacobs wrote, "Dark the world is, even with God. Without Him, dark and light both lose their ultimate meaning." Everyone, even the believer, has moments of doubt. But the whole of man's history has been a struggle with God. There were times of greater faith, times of lesser faith. But when believers most wanted to reject God they did not cast Him out. They argued, but they did not abdicate. If today people claim to deny Him out of conviction and not from cowardice, that does not justify reading their position back into history and saying, "If God is dead, it's because He never lived." What does the secular humanist call the universal feeling that there are realms above and beyond the earthbound and mundane? How do they handle life's mystery and mystique, its transcendent and spiritual? The Jewish pietists known as Hassidim say that the person who feels far from God is nearer to Him than they know. The person who is searching for righteousness and justice may be walking with God even without mentioning His name, even without admitting that He is there beside them.

24. *Goodness*

Good God! Be a good boy! Goodness gracious me! Goodonyer! Apart from the last example, which only Australians will understand (it's a contraction of "Good on you!") these phrases are part of our daily speech. Everybody talks about goodness, though not everybody wants to be good. St. Augustine said when he was not quite ready for saintliness, "God, make me good—but not yet!" Leo Hebraeus said in the Middle Ages that there were three kinds of goodness—the profitable, the pleasurable, and the virtuous. The first category is expedient: it brings you benefit; it's good for your purse. The second category is sensual: it gives you enjoyment; it's good for your feelings. Both categories are selfish. It's the third category that's unselfish. Virtuous goodness is altruistic, its own reward. The virtuously good person believes in the right thing and does it. The right thing is virtuous; the virtuous thing is right. You can play with these words for ever. Without an idea of what "virtuous" and "right" really mean you get nowhere. They both entail moral excellence, following the highest standards of ethical values. Not ostentatiously, not by advertising your qualities (remember Dickens' Uriah Heep who wanted everyone to know how 'umble he was?), but by being like Moses who "knew not that his face shone". You see goodness on a good person's face but if you say so you'll be told, "What, me? I'm no saint—I just try to do the right thing!" Good people endear themselves to others. As a colleague once told me, "It's nice to be good, but it's good to be nice". Goodness and niceness seem to go together.

25. Gratitude

When Moses had to bring the Ten Plagues on the ancient Egyptians he refused to be involved in anything that would harm the River Nile. It would be ungrateful since the river had sheltered him as a baby. If one can show gratitude to a river, one can show it to anyone (including God) and anything, even to a place or moment. There are times and places—and experiences and ideas—that make all the difference to everyone's life, and years afterwards their influence is still felt. Old-fashioned etiquette dictated that a letter or card of thanks should go to a host or hostess, and though the letter- or card-writing habit may be more or less extinct it is still important to find a way to say "Thankyou". One should also never forget to thank God for His bounty. The Psalmist says, "The lines have fallen for me in pleasant places" (Psalm 16). All the pleasant things in life can be traced ultimately to Divine blessings. Count your own blessings and learn to say "Thankyou, God!" Further, in gratitude for what God has given you, find ways of bringing your own blessings to other people.

26. *Greatness*

How do you become a great person? You don't go looking for it. If it happens, it happens. There is a proverb that is thought to be in the Talmud but isn't: "Whoever chases after honour, honour flees from him. Whoever flees from honour, honour pursues him." Since some people are widely recognised as great, how did they get there if they were not meant to chase after greatness? The truth is that some really did chase after it. When a youngster was interviewed for a position, the manager asked him, "What is your ambition?" He said: "To have your job!" Eventually he did become manager and then chairman of directors, but that's probably unusual. To become great, you have to prove your energy, your ability, your perseverance. At the beginning we hope people will say, "He's a fine young man!" Later they will say, "He is doing allright". Next they will say, "He is doing exceptionally well". Eventually the highest compliment will come: "He's incredible!" It won't always be a fairy story like this because not everybody is fair and generous with their praise. Some are mean, some feel threatened, some don't like your shoes, your spouse, or the sound of your voice, and all this will impede your progress. But greatness doesn't have to be measured by your office or title. It's not *where* you are but *who* you are.

27. *Guilt*

"It's all my fault. How can I get over my feelings of guilt?" You can't, whether the guilt is genuine or you are masochistically punishing yourself. The real question is how you face up to your guilt and live with it. The best way is to try to make amends, preferably without a song and dance, but that's not always possible. What *is* always possible is to use the guilt constructively instead of obsessing, recognising where you went wrong (or think you did) and using that knowledge to do right. If you sinned with your words, use your mouth to speak positively to and about other people. If you sinned with your feet, maybe by going to places where you shouldn't have been, use your feet to walk towards good causes, to keep company with good people. If you sinned with your money, become a generous supporter of those who need help. If you sinned against God, try to listen more attentively to His Word.

If you sinned against your own better self, don't tear yourself apart by minimising your self-worth. Say to yourself, "I am fundamentally a decent person; I can and will pick myself up and do better in future". It is said that when Jacob Epstein was a boy he crushed a bird to death in his hands. Using his shame and guilt constructively he used his hands to become a famous sculptor and to be knighted as Sir Jacob Epstein.

28. *Hands*

"Hand" is the handiest word in the dictionary—handwork, handcart, handicraft, handover, hand-me-down, handkerchief, secondhand . . . the list is endless. The hands are the busiest part of the body. No wonder we are taught to wash our hands because of all the things they might have touched. According to Psalm 24, "clean hands and a pure heart" are the way to "ascend the mountain of the Lord and stand in His holy place". In this sense "clean" is a metaphor; Isaiah, in Chapter 1, criticises those whose "hands are full of blood". Hands are so intricate, so versatile, that they can achieve immensely important results, but only if they are clean is the result morally significant. If they are dirty and filled with blood they will be the cause of violence and harm, literally "weapons of mass destruction". This explains why shaking hands is a mode of greeting—producing your hands showed that your intentions were peaceful with no weapons hidden in your sleeve. The dual capacity of the hands is also illustrated by the words of Ben Sira in the Apocrypha, "Let not your hands be stretched out to take but closed when it's time to give". The hands should work together. As the Gospel of Matthew says, your left hand should know (and approve) what your right hand does. Otherwise, if one hand serves the cause of good and the other the cause of evil, it's nothing but hypocrisy.

29. *Happiness*

Is happiness the same as contentment? The Biblical word for happy, *ashrei,* is actually plural. It's a collective noun because happiness is different things to different people. It can be emotional—a feeling of exhilaration and delight. Or psychological—a feeling of satisfaction.

According to Samson Raphael Hirsch in the 19th century, happiness is having a direction in life, a purpose, a goal. Conan Doyle might have summed it up when he put into Sherlock Holmes' mouth the words, "Watson, the game is afoot!" When the game is afoot, you're embarked on something exciting. Whichever concept you choose, happiness is both passive and active. *Passive*, in that you are suffused with the feeling that, in Browning's words, "God's in his heaven, all's right with the world". *Active*, in that you are on the move and every fibre of your being is tingling with joy. You are amazed at how happy you feel. It sounds like C.S. Lewis' book, "Surprised by Joy", which the Psalms anticipated when they said (Chapter 30), "Joy cometh in the morning". I have quoted so many people in this chapter that I hope you will let me quote another, the philosopher Franz Rosenzweig, who said, "Happiness and life are two different things, and it's no wonder that men come to ascribe bliss to the dead alone". I'm glad Rosenzweig used the word "bliss" because it's another synonym for happiness, but I can't agree that you're only happy when you're dead. The thought is too morbid; I don't think it is true.

30. *Health*

Health is connected with "hale". When you're *hale and hearty* you're in good overall physical, mental and psychological shape. You, and your doctor, should be concerned with the whole person, not just the body as a collection of spare parts. You, and the doctor, should also recognise that overall health depends on lifestyle and not just medication. When everything is in working order and functions as part of the whole, you will feel well. My Jewish tradition is probably unique amongst religious faiths in that it has a prayer to be recited after using the toilet, praising the Creator for having placed our soul in an intricate bodily structure in which when everything opens and closes as necessary, one's life can function. It is one of God's greatest miracles that our various parts interact so efficiently. It is also a Divine miracle that the medical profession can be God's partners in bringing healing when it becomes necessary. When you watch the hospital programmes on television you possibly squirm and avert your eyes at scenes in the operating theatre, involving all that blood and guts. Fair enough, but what a wondrous gift it is to belong to the healing professions.

31. History

According to Henry Ford, history is "just bunk". It's a good job that no historian has retorted by saying that cars—especially Fords—are just bunk. Historians have more sense than to talk such nonsense. Whatever has happened not only deserves to be recalled for its sheer interest, but because we need to know where we came from and to learn from it (though Bernard Shaw remarked that what we learn from history is that we don't). Old-timers sometimes wish that history had never happened—or rather, that the past could be repeated. It's like A.A. Milne writing about a child who says, "I think I'll stay six for ever and ever". Very nice, but staying six for ever isn't fair to other people: they deserve a chance to have a go at life. It's also not fair to yourself: you need to experience every stage in life and not be frozen at six or any other age. Forget about the "good old days". The Bible warns, "Say not 'the former days were better'" (Ecclesiastes Chapter 7). Would we really like to be in an era when medicine was much less advanced, when hardly anybody reached a ripe old age, infant mortality was horrendous, sanitation primitive and communications poor, and humanity had not yet developed the wonders of the modern world? I know it's no great deal to be enveloped in the fear and uncertainty that are caused by modern methods of torture and terror, but that's no excuse for being like Lot's wife and wanting to turn back. Our challenge is to look at history and improve on it as we construct the future. Martin Buber says, "The past of (one's) people is his personal memory: the future is his personal task."

32. Holiness

People can be holy. So can words, places, deeds, moments, books. Ask people what "holy" means and you're likely to be told "sacred", but that's just a synonym. The underlying idea is "different, special, out of the ordinary"—with an additional factor. Holiness inhabits a higher, spiritual plane. Some religions believe it requires you to withdraw from the contamination of the outside world, to retreat into a spiritual shell, to isolate yourself from the mundane. That's a mistake. The real test of holiness is whether you can work and move in the ordinary world and still maintain your dignity and standards. In Leviticus Chapter 19, God asks humans to be holy . . . and then proceeds to talk about family relationships, running a business and other commonplace activities. The mark of holiness is whether you can make the ordinary extraordinary, live in the community and not lose your faith, talk to others and keep your speech clean, face temptation and have nerves of moral steel. You probably won't get any votes of thanks for your holiness. People may not even notice you. But your core values will be safe, your conscience will be clear, and you can face God. Holiness is not just how you pray but how you play, not just your worship but your worthiness. You will lapse once in a while, because the pressures are usually extreme—but holiness is also the moral courage to dust yourself off and try to rise high once more. You don't have to be an angel in order to be holy, but you do have to be the best possible kind of human being.

33. *Honesty*

Sunday School children used to learn hymns about ethics. I don't know the words of the one about honesty, but the hymn about truth was, "Be the matter what it may, always tell the truth". Many subjects used to be taught in song: that's how I learnt Latin grammar. The Bible often summed up ethical teachings in short, pithy sayings. Concerning honesty it spoke about just weights and measures ("just" = honest, fair and correct. No-one should cheat anyone else or want to). I don't know whether one is born with a sense of honesty or whether it grows—that's the old nature/nurture debate. I do know that some people don't start with honesty but adopt it when they've moved beyond dishonesty (their policy is "Get on, get honour, get honest"). When a certain land proposed a law against counterfeit money a wise man said, "What—a law against counterfeit money? You must be a scoundrel if you need such a law to keep you honest!" Honesty applies far beyond money matters. Without it nobody will ever be a good husband or wife: marriages have to be built on trust. Without it nobody will ever be a scholar or scientist: the facts must never be twisted or distorted. With all the terrorism and errorism in today's world the media ought not sell their soul to the devil. When I told that to a media conference I got a standing ovation, but the next day nothing had changed. The Talmud says that the first question at the gateway to heaven is, "Were you honest in your dealings with others?"

34. *Honour*

English is a strange language. Sometimes you sound an "h" and sometimes you don't. Someone who picked up English as an adult had constant problems with "h" words. He complained of "ay fever" because he didn't know that "hay" has a sounded "h" (what would he would have made of the Australian slang about the town of Hay, "It's 'ot as 'ell in 'ay"?) and he thought that "honour" was two words, "Oh nor". Did he realise that the American spelling is "honor"? More important, though, than the spelling and pronunciation is the concept. To honour is to respect and look up to. The Ten Commandments tell us to honour our parents. Thring, the great headmaster of Uppingham, told his students, "Honour the work and the work will honour you". Citizens of all nations are constantly enjoined to honour their people's tradition, flag and leaders. But there's a converse. The leaders of nations and national movements often show no honour to their own citizens and mistreat their own people. How many supposed leaders keep calling for their adherents to honour them despite their feet of clay? Harold Laski, the political scientist, said that states and human beings "never protest their honour loudly unless they have a bad case to argue". One of the highest forms of honour is the honour of self—not as an exaggerated boast about one's greatness but a fair appreciation of one's talents and worth.

35. *Hope*

Lovely dreams. *I hope* I will win the lottery. *I hope* the neighbours will move out. *I hope* the TV will show the cricket a bit earlier. It's nice to dream, but one's hopes ought to be more realistic. Viscount Herbert

Samuel, philosopher as well as politician, mused about optimism (an abundance of hope) and pessimism (a shortage of hope) and asked himself what he was—an optimist or a pessimist. He decided that he was a *meliorist* (from the Latin for "better"). He believed that on the whole things were getting better and he would try to make them continue to do so. This conclusion moved hope from the arena of ethereal dreaming and turned it into a shrewd assessment of the facts and a pragmatic determination to work on them. A view which connects with Antonio Gramsci, who urged "pessimism of the intellect, optimism of the will". In simple terms this seems to say, "Fear the worst, work for the best". In that sense hope is a practical notion, a spur to action, the ability to believe that action can lead to meaningful change. The Israelite slaves in ancient Egypt already won a moral victory when they refused to abandon their values and standards. All downtrodden peoples were already triumphant when they kept up their hope in a better future. Their suffering could so easily have snuffed out even the thought of hope. But they did more than just dream. They hitched their wagon to a star and slowly moved upwards towards a better day. It took decades, even generations or centuries, but the dawn finally arrived.

36. *Hospitality*

There is a legend that Abraham, the ancient patriarch, had doors on all four sides of his house to save guests the trouble of searching for the entrance when they sought hospitality. It is also said that he served his guests personally, offered them lodging overnight, and accompanied them part of the way when they departed. No wonder people said, "Blessed be the God of Abraham". In medieval France, hospitable people had their coffins made from the wood of the tables where they had served their guests. Some pious people emblazoned above their doors the words from the Book of Job Chapter 31: "The stranger shall not stay in the street: I will open my doors to the wanderer". There is a common idea that hospitality is basically for the benefit of the guest, but it goes both ways. The host gets to know interesting people; new friendships are made, the world comes right into one's doors. The memory of the time spent together can last for a lifetime—on both sides. When I came to London as a student I had invitations that left such enjoyable memories that years later I can still taste the food! There are two ways of showing gratitude for hospitality. One is saying or writing a proper "Thankyou"; the other is making a personal and family habit of hospitality.

37. *Humility*

Ben Sira says in the Apocrypha, "The greater you are, the more you should humble yourself—then you will find favour before the Lord." How does this work in practice? A king was told that a man of humility is rewarded with long life. The king attired himself in old garments, moved into a small hut, and forbade anyone to show him reverence. But when he honestly examined himself the king found himself to be prouder of his seeming humility than he ever was of his greatness. Thereupon a sage remarked to him, "Vanity destroys humility. Dress like a king, live like a king, but be humble in your innermost heart." A humble heart means humility towards God: "God: I may be a king, but You are the King of Kings". Humility towards people: "God: You have given me a chance to rule over Your children; please help me to put their wellbeing before my own". It also means humility towards yourself: "God: I am basically the same as everyone else; please make me worthy of my blessings". One of the Hassidic masters said, "Everybody should have two pockets. In one should be a piece of paper with the verse, 'I am just earth and ashes'; in the other, 'For my sake was the world created'. He should dip into one or the other according to his needs." We all need a dose of each. The secret is to find out how much each dose should be.

38. *Justice*

London's Strand has a Victorian-style building called The Supreme Court of Justice. With all due respect to my learned friends in the law, what the judges administer is not justice, but law. Law is a reality, justice is an ideal. Sometimes law gets near to justice but the ideal remains elusive. A verse in the Bible (Deuteronomy Chapter 16) tells us, "Justice, justice shall you pursue"—pursue it even though you may never quite get there. There is distributive justice, the fair allocation of rights and duties. There is retributive justice, "good for good, evil for evil". A third category is substantive justice. In Biblical literature that third kind of justice occurs often—in company with love, charity, peace, integrity and redemption. It is a code word for a sound, wholesome community, where the law achieves a happy climate for everyone. Utopian? Bernard Shaw said, "Let those who may complain that it was all on paper remember that only on paper has humanity yet achieved glory, beauty, truth, knowledge, virtue and abiding love". True, but by putting the ideals on paper we have taken a useful first step. Once that step has been taken we can get to work to bring it into being and build a society in which, to quote the Bible again, "justice shall well up like waters and righteousness as the mighty stream" (Amos, Chapter 5).

39. *Language*

Human beings started to talk from the moment the world was created, and they still haven't stopped. The power of speech brings immense good to civilisation, and immense harm. The way people twist words and manipulate the crowds is an indication of how dangerous language can be. Not only in the hands (or the mouths) of dictators and demagogues. Ordinary people are far from models of virtue in this—and other—respects. Their worst sins are the little ones committed with their tongues. "Mind your tongue!" was one of the first lessons we learned as small children. Those who were sensible soon learnt that it is better to say nothing than to say the wrong thing. Those who were less sensible were warned, "If you use bad language I'll wash your mouth out with soap," and some parents actually did exactly that, though whether it was hard soap or liquid soap has not been recorded. The problem is that in recent decades the attempts to control smutty language have abysmally failed. Modern culture hankers after the bizarre in everything and the words you hear all the time on the television and in daily speech are precisely those that our parents tried to eradicate. Moses Maimonides said in the Middle Ages that things that are noble can be said in any language and things that are not noble should not be said at all.

40. *Laughter*

Humour is very important. Not everything has to be serious or solemn. There is a funny side to everything. There is even a droll side to tragedy when you cry and laugh at the same time: there is a book called "Laughter in Hell" about Holocaust humour, which pokes fun at the enemy. It quotes Natan Sharansky: "In freedom, humour is a mere luxury. In prison, it's the only weapon". It laughs amid its tears, it cries amid its jokes. Even God resorts to humour; without it He would also probably want to cry. In the Book of Psalms you hear Him laughing at the pretensions of human beings (see Psalm 2). According to Professor John Benson, who wrote a study of the subject, "God's humour seems to delight in laying low the haughty, in humiliating the arrogant." There is an intellectual side to humour: Freud said that a joke has two qualities—it makes us laugh and it serves our ideological interest. Sometimes humour is rather cruel. Fortunately, it is often rather good-natured. A.P. Herbert, no mean humorist, said that if you tell me what you laugh at I will know who you are and where you fit in. Yet laughter is not necessarily the same as humour. When you laugh there may not be anything particularly funny about it. Laughter—like a baby's gurgle at seeing its mother—is a sign of delight and pleasure. When there is laughter in a house it is sure to be a home of happiness.

41. *Leadership*

What makes a leader? Belief in the cause ("It's a vital cause and it's achievable"). Belief in the team ("We make a good crew"). Belief in the rank and file ("They're good people and they'll back me"). Inspiration ("I'll help them dream dreams and see visions"). Articulateness ("I am good with words"). Self-confidence ("I do some things particularly well"). Integrity ("They can trust me"). Stamina ("I can outlast the hurdles"). Determination ("I'll see it through"). Modesty ("I'm good but I know I'm not perfect"). Altruism ("I'm not here to serve myself but the cause"). Leadership is hard on you: you are blamed for everything and you get less than your fair share of credit. Leadership brings its agonies, and you have to rise above them; it brings its ecstasies, and you mustn't get a swelled head. You'll have your doubts and feel tempted to give it all away, but you have to keep going. You'll have setbacks and you'll lose a few battles, but you have to salvage what you can, and re-group. All true leadership often fails—like Moses, you may never get to the Promised Land. It also mostly succeeds, even if you won't be there to see it—like Moses, you know that Joshua will keep the flag flying. So why be a leader? Because it's exhilarating to pursue a cause and to do what only you can do.

42. Leisure

A French writer speaks of the culture of the picnic. He doesn't mean that all of life is a picnic. The poet says, "Life is real, life is earnest". But we need time out. This is the idea of the weekly Sabbath. Ben Sira, a provocative author in the Apocrypha, says that wisdom comes with leisure. Leisure not only works on the body but on the mind—a time for recreation and for re-creation. Some people play hard sport, others go hiking in the fresh air, others curl up in front of the fire with a good book. Me, I like star-gazing, in a metaphorical sense—a chance to let my mind roam. Life's distractions tend to crowd out the serious ideas. Some people may be happier that way. Israel Abrahams said, "Children are afraid of the dark; we are afraid of the light". Though Socrates says, "Know thyself!" many people prefer not to. It's an important art to get your ideas in order. I do it when I'm reading. I turn myself off—often during a religious service—and go into a private reverie. Sometimes it is sparked by a word, a phrase, and image that leaps out of the page. One thing suggests another, and off I go. I only come back to the world when people stand up. I stand up too—an automatic reflex—but I stand better because I've had my time out. I used to like jogging: I still enjoy brisk walking but most of all I dream and discover myself.

43. Life

We decide many things for ourselves, but life, the biggest thing of all, is beyond our control. No-one asks whether we want to be born, nor do we get a say as to who our parents will be. At the other end of life we also have very little control: in most cases we neither choose nor even know when we will die. The prophet Jonah had his moments when he wanted to opt out of life. Things had not gone the way he wanted and he thought that, on the whole, non-living was preferable to living. Probably most of us have times when we share that feeling, but fortunately by the next day we have come to terms with being alive and discovered that it has its good points after all. There is a wise saying of Andre Maurois: "Life is too short to be little". Think over the next quotation—it comes from the Talmud—and see if it doesn't lead you to the same conclusion: "Maybe it would have been better if man had not been created, but since he has been created, let him work on his deeds". You only get one chance at living so you might as well make the most of it and not make your life too "little". You never really know the meaning of life but you might as well live as if it were something really worthwhile and precious. Justice Louis Brandeis commented rather cynically, "I have only one life, and it is short enough. Why waste it on things I don't want most?"

44. Light

Cecil Rhodes' last words were "*Mehr Licht*—more light!" Whatever he had in mind at that moment, we can all echo the sentiments. We often feel that more light would improve our lives, since there is so much darkness and gloom in today's environment. But it would be unrealistic to yearn for constant light and joy. Life is a kaleidoscope; there are bound to be bad times as well as good. This is not to suggest that we should pray for bad times—they have a habit of turning up on their own. The art is to endure the bad times and never lose faith in the coming of joy. It is comforting to be told in the Psalms (Chapter 30), "Weeping tarries for the night but joy comes in the morning"—if only we could be certain that the night would not go on too long! Not everybody suffers in the same way at the same time and when we see others in the midst of darkness we can often light up their lives by a smile or even just by being there when we are most needed. Every religion probably has its festival of light and one of the most religious things we can do is to be generous in sharing our light.

45. Loneliness

Balaam and Jonah are Biblical characters whom history has misunderstood because of an animal. Balaam is overshadowed by his talking donkey, and Jonah by being inside a big fish (not a whale, despite the popular view). Actually both are fascinating characters in themselves. Jonah has already figured in this book so let's talk about Balaam. When the going got tough he went to "a bare height" (Numbers 23). He wanted to be alone to think things through. Franz Kafka said, "You do not need to leave your room. Remain sitting at your table and listen. Do not even listen: simply wait". So why does Genesis (Chapter 2) say, "It is not good for a person to be alone"? Some kinds of aloneness are good, some aren't. It's not good to feel abandoned and friendless. That makes two kinds of aloneness, voluntary and involuntary, but there is a third: existential aloneness. According to the Swiss thinker Henri Frederic Amiel, "In all the chief matters of life we are alone: we dream alone, we die alone". Even with others by our side, our existential aloneness cannot be shared. Balaam's was voluntary aloneness. He needed to be on his own without noise or distraction. The outcome was the aloneness of moral courage. Even if it cost him the king's support, he had to speak up and say what had to be said. Others might have urged him not to go out on a limb for the sake of an ideal, but he knew there were times to stand alone even if the rest of the world was opposed or indifferent.

46. Love

It's a deep feeling, a stage beyond liking. Liking does not have to develop into loving, but when it does, you know you have both arrived. Unfortunately, the definitions of love are all severely limited. An example: "Love is never having to say sorry" . . . but the truth is the opposite. If there is love, you each have to be able to be and say sorry, because you must be able to trust one another. Another definition, an improvement on the first: "Love is the engagement of the heart" . . . agreed, but true love engages every part of your being. "Love is empathy" . . . true enough, but not good enough. In the Bible we are told to love God and our fellow man. Fine, but the motivation is important—sometimes it is "I love you so you will love me". That's expedient love, but better is "I love you for your own sake". The test is suggested by Moshe Leib of Sassov: "If you truly love me, you know where I hurt." It is said that absence makes the heart grow fonder, but a better idea is, "I can't bear to be separated from you"—with the rather morbid corollary suggested by Morris Adler, that sorrow is the reverse side of love: when you say "I love you" you are on the way to eventually having to part. When you say "Hello" you risk one day having to say "Goodbye". What really matters is what happens *in between* the "Hello" and "Goodbye", how much joy you can bring each other in between meeting and parting.

47. *Loyalty*

"I fed you bread and you threw back stones". One person told me this was a Hungarian saying, another thought it was from the New Testament. Whatever the source, it is a fair summing up of disloyalty. Loyalty is reliability: sticking by a person or a cause. "I knew I could depend on you and you wouldn't let me down"—that's loyalty. Being a friend means that you're not just there in fair weather. Being a supporter means that they can count on you. It was a mark of the founding fathers of the United States, who, according to Arthur M. Schlesinger, quoted by Barbara Tuchman in "The March of Folly: From Troy to Vietnam", were "fearless, high-principled, deeply versed in ancient and modern political thought, astute and pragmatic, unafraid of experiment, and . . . convinced of man's power to improve his condition through the use of intelligence". Loyalty can take many forms. One can have multiple loyalties. Justice Louis Brandeis said, "Multiple loyalties are objectionable only if they are inconsistent". At one and the same time you can owe fidelity to your family, your sports club, your political party, your professional association, your religious community . . . and so many other identities, Very rarely do you have to decide between them. You can also feel loyal to more than one country, and you can hold more than one passport.

48. Man

"What a piece of work is man!" said Shakespeare. I say, what a piece of mystery is man. In the North of England they say, "There's nowt so strange as folks". Man is a parcel of paradoxes—sometimes an angel, sometimes a beast; often kind and generous, frequently mean and selfish; thirsting for the ethereal heavens, sometimes wallowing in the muddy slime. Heine calls him the aristocrat among animals, but he can also be the animal amongst aristocrats. Sometimes he finds answers, sometimes he can't even ask the right questions. At his best, man is unique and incomparable. Though man is a social being, Leo Baeck says that he is the only creature that is aware of his individuality. Alone amongst the Divine creations, man has a sense of history; another of Leo Baeck's observations is that man is the only creature that knows of his grandparents and his grandchildren. Yet a medieval poet says, "Man—thirst in his throat, fear in his heart, sin in his lap, hate in his growth". But man has his uses. It is only the beginning of the truth to say, as Spinoza did, "To man there is nothing more useful than man". We have to continue the thought and add, "To God too, there is nothing more useful than man". What's really great about man is that he is the only creature who worries about who he is and where he is going.

49. Miracles

Miracles are exceptions to the rules—a philosophical quandary for the pedants who work so hard to understand the structure of the universe and find that the structure doesn't always work because something constantly pops out of its box. Theology can handle the problem by means of the doctrine that even the exceptions are capable of being categorised and analysed. The believer blessed with a poet's soul will say that sometimes God even surprises Himself with His miracles. The student of humanity will say that sometimes we surprise God with *our* miracles when we reach beyond the norms. It is said that David Ben Gurion asked Chief Rabbi Herzog, "Why doesn't God send us a miracle?" . . . and the rabbi replied, "He does, and the miracle is you!" Another great rabbi, the Lubavitcher Rebbe, fell ill with chest pains and eight heart specialists were called. The rabbi's supporters prayed hard, but the Rebbe did not expect God to act instead of the doctors. If we ask why God did not send a miracle during the Holocaust, surely He did try; He hoped human beings would themselves be the miracle and would speak up and act to save the victims, but almost everybody failed to live up to their miraculous potentialities. Every day humanity could, if it wished, achieve miracles more amazing than any in history.

50. Money

Tevye's sour comment in "Fiddler on the Roof" is "Money is a curse—I wish You'd curse me with more of it". When is money a curse? When you are consumed by it. When you want it more than friends, family or health. When you want it all for yourself. Someone said, "Money is a wonderful thing, but it is possible to pay too high a price for it". When it goes to your head it's a curse. Psalm 49 warns us, though in different words, "You can't take it with you" There are people who think they're the greatest because they have money, and there are less affluent people who think the others are right. When is money not a curse? When you recognise you'll never be a millionaire but are still busy and cheerful. When you use constructively whatever you've got. There's an old question: "What would you do if you won the lottery?" One answer: "I'd give it to my children" (don't worry—they'll happily take it but maybe you should keep some for yourself). The preacher's answer: "My sermons would be different" (I hope not—if you preach the right things already it shouldn't matter how much you have). A German author wrote, "To acquire money requires valour, to keep money requires prudence, to spend money well is an art".

51. Night

There are several claimants for the title of The City That Never Sleeps. To them, night is day and day is night. What others do in daytime they do at night. Presumably they sleep during the day. Most other people think sleeping is a night-time event. That makes the night a valuable resource, time to wind down, to overcome today and build strength for tomorrow. In that sense it's far from a non-event. Not that that's its only value. Night is when it's quiet and if you're awake you can do some thinking. Paradoxically you can also day-dream. Most of us can't day-dream during the day because we're surrounded by noise and bustle and can't step off the treadmill. Before I retired and my life changed, the people in the pews didn't quite know what to make of my advice to sit at a worship service and ignore what was going on, to shut yourself off from the prayers and professions of piety and dream about who you are and what you're doing with your life. Very few ever told me that they'd tried it because they didn't think that's what clergymen should be telling them. My advice does work, because I've tried it and it's one of the few chances of having a successful day-dream. King David is said to have hung a harp over his bed which played at midnight and woke the king for meditation and study. In later history some Jewish pietists made sure they rose at midnight to weep and pray for the rebuilding of the Temple in Jerusalem. To them that would symbolise the end of centuries of dark ages, when all of life was an unending night-time.

52. Old Age

Our span of life is increasing. People are living much longer. Many will reach a ripe old age, whatever that phrase means. Though the Bible (Leviticus 19) says, "Rise before the hoary head" and Israeli buses reserve the front seats for hoary-headers, nobody is sure any more what a hoary head is. If it denotes grey or white hair, what about bald people? If it is a matter of age, why is 70 what lawyers call statutory senility, when most people over 70 are still crisp in their minds? It's not just what society has to say but how the ageing person thinks of him- or herself. Some people still play sport or engage in other physical activity in their 80s or 90s—good luck to them; others simply say, "I'm not even tempted". Some sink into anecdotage and live with stories from the past. Don't laugh at them; they are valuable living historians. There are other things too that are still possible at an age which some see as God's waiting-room. Moses was still working at 120. History would have been the poorer without a number of fully productive leaders who refused to be shunted aside at 70 or 80. Not everyone is creative at 90, but nor are some people at 30 or 40. There is no reason to say, "Make way for the young", nor "You're a has-been". Sometimes the elderly are more reliable and creative than their juniors. Some cultures worship their ancestors: we shouldn't worship our descendants.

53. *Peace*

Peace has always been mankind's supreme ideal: look up Micah and Isaiah. Now however the word is so over-used, especially when combined with "process" ("the peace process"), that it has been emptied of all meaning. The Hebrew "*Shalom*" is linked with *sh'lemut*, "completeness". Peace is when everything is complete, in its place and in order. The thrush and nightingale once defined peace. This is the story. There was a meeting of the animals and birds in the forest. The lion announced that they all had to heed his word because he was the king and he could roar much louder than the rest of them combined. To prove it he emitted such a roar that the other creatures jumped with fright. After the echo had died down the little thrush said quietly, "Yes, King Lion, you really can roar louder than anyone else, but your voice is only strong at the beginning. It gets weaker and fainter the further away one is. A mile away or so no-one can hear you at all. Compared to you my voice is much weaker, but when I begin to sing, the nightingale and all the other birds join in, and after a few moments the whole forest is alive with the sound of music." What does this tell us about peace? The way to peace is not by emitting a big roar that scares everyone else, but through "little" people sharing the music of harmony. The way to peace is people-to-people more than lion-to-lion or tiger-to-tiger.

54. *Pleasure*

God filled the world with pleasurable things. That's the message of the Book of Ecclesiastes, sounding suspiciously like Greek hedonism. It says, "There is nothing better than to rejoice and get pleasure as long as one lives" (Chapter 3). It adds, "I recommend mirth, for a person has no better thing under the sun than to eat, drink and be merry" (Chapter 8). Others are more restrained. Proverbs says, "He who loves pleasure will come to want" (Chapter 21). Philo, the philosopher of

Alexandria, sadly remarked, "Nothing ever escapes desire, but like a forest fire it proceeds onward, consuming and destroying everything". With so much ambivalence what are we to do? Eat, drink and be merry, or sit, starve and mope? All these classical statements seem to agree that eating, drinking, money, music, entertainment and sex are the ingredients of pleasure (though our modern age would add a few more items, some as innocent as cruising and others more exotic and bizarre). We probably need to conclude that if God allowed them into His world they were meant to be there and are not necessarily evil in themselves—but they have to be disciplined and kept within bounds. Too much pleasure-seeking and we become a sad, over-sated picture. A little of what you fancy does you good, but too much becomes a consuming fire.

55. Popularity

Television dramas are full of the chase after popularity. Everyone seems to be obsessed with the subject. If no-one likes you there's something wrong, though maybe they're using the wrong criteria: perhaps they're judging the whole you because of your clothes or hairdo. If everyone likes you there can also be a problem: maybe they don't like you for yourself but for some benefit that comes from being in your circle. There is a New Testament passage in the Gospel of Luke (Chapter 6) that warns, "Woe unto you when all men shall speak well of you!" You can try to court popularity but there's no guarantee that you won't feel ashamed of yourself later. Though there's a poem by Heine that goes something like this: "Write for the mob, not for posterity—then will the people deify you", your self-respect will suffer if you serve the mob for the sake of the momentary plaudits. The best thing is to stick to your conscience and even if the mob disapproves, at least it gives you a greater chance of approving of yourself. Nonetheless it doesn't do any harm to have an open hand and a smile on your face and to be thoughtful and friendly to others. Unfortunately, however, you'll never please all of the people all of the time. Oscar Levant, the American pianist-composer, said, "I'm a controversial figure. My friends either dislike me or hate me".

56. Power

There are two ways of exerting power—through political action, and through ethical influence. The ancient Greeks thought the two should be combined: kings should be sages and sages should be kings. Experience should have taught them, as Will Herberg said, that "the disinterested devotion to truth and goodness implied by philosophy does not go well with the relativities of interest and expediency", and that grand ideals and visions become tainted if enmeshed with power politics. Power politics seem to require expediency and compromise. The pragmatic realities of running an institution or a State require accommodating a range of pressures and militate against wise, high-minded, altruistic idealism. Lord Acton's famous words were, "Power corrupts: absolute power corrupts absolutely". Many great figures in history refused to accept public office and preferred to exert an influence behind the scenes. Nevertheless there is still a need for political figures who symbolise and administer the rule of law—who was it who said that without rulers the populace would eat each other alive? Ideally power and influence would work together; every institution or State would have a moral ombudsman capable enough of assessing the way power is used, credible enough to be heeded and heard.

57. Praise

What a strange phrase, "Praise the Lord and pass the ammunition". Out of context it doesn't amount to much. In normal circumstances who would think of God and ammunition in the same breath? True, in today's crazy world some people believe in holy wars and attack others whilst invoking the name of the Deity, but I'd prefer people to love each other in the name of God and not use Him as an excuse for mayhem and murder. Praise should be given to God for life, love and light, for beauty, brains and benevolence, for humanity, health and humour. Praise should be given to other people for enriching the Creation, arousing the human heart and stretching the human mind. If others have also wrought acts of evil, forgive them and try to teach them better. Should we praise ourselves too, for our own achievements and qualities? We should certainly appreciate ourselves and remember that Erich Fromm said that loving oneself is as necessary as loving our neighbour, though it's folly to look in the mirror and say, "Aren't I the greatest!" The Book of Proverbs says (Chapter 27), "Let another praise you, not your own mouth". If others are slow to praise you, let your deeds be their own praise; Proverbs also says (Chapter 31), "Let her works praise her in the gates" and Ben Sira says in the Apocrypha, "The work praises its master". But don't do things in the hope of praise: do the right thing for its own sake and thank God for your abilities.

58. *Prayer*

If things are good, prayer says, "May they remain so"; if they're not so good, prayer says, "May they improve".

The Biblical word for prayer is from a root that means to judge. In prayer I judge myself—what I have, what I need, who I am.

Prayer says that my blessings have a Source—God. My destiny has a Supervisor—God. My task is as a partner—with God.

Did I work this out logically? That's Reason. Did it come to me? That's Revelation. Did I just know? That's Instinct.

Does prayer do me any good? It makes me appreciate life and the world more. Sometimes it brings something I asked for. Not always—perhaps the answer was No, perhaps I was selfish and what I wanted wouldn't be good for the rest of the world, perhaps I was asking something unworthy or trivial.

Prayer is good for you. Alexis Carrel says: "Prayer stamps with its indelible mark our actions and demeanour. A tranquillity of bearing, a facial and bodily repose, are observed in those whose inner lives are thus enriched. Within the depths of consciousness a flame kindles. A man sees himself. He discovers his selfishness, his silly pride, his fears, his greeds, his blunders. He develops a sense of moral obligation, intellectual humility."

I cannot help praying. Levi Yitzhak of Berditchev observed a thief taking a clock. "What a clever man!" he said, "He wants to know when to pray".

59. Rain

What comes down in the rain has intrigued the poets from time immemorial Is it cats and dogs? That particular notion probably originates in Jonathan Swift's writings. Is it violets? I don't know who thought that one up. Probably what they're getting at is the contrast between pelting rainstorms and gentle showers. There's poetry in rain whichever way you look at it—that is, unless you're caught in a deluge and get drenched. If that happens you aren't interested in poetry as much as an umbrella. The Jewish sages were smart when they looked at a verse in Deuteronomy Chapter 11, "I will give rain for your land in its season". "Rain for your land" means irrigation, growth, vegetation, food, prosperity. "In its season", they say, means the Sabbath evening when everyone is at home and no-one will get drenched in the streets. In this way you get the benefits of the rain without its drawbacks. There are some parts of the world where it teems and then—all of a sudden—you get beautiful sun as if God is teasing you from Heaven. One minute you need an umbrella and the next moment a parasol. It would suit human beings to be able to control the climate in order to get just enough sun and just enough rain, but then most people wouldn't have anything to talk about. Imagine sitting in a taxi and being unable to discuss the weather. You might have to talk about politics or religion.

60. Reading

Reading and literacy are not identical. Literacy is a technical skill. Reading is the way one uses that skill and opens new vistas of enjoyment and knowledge. Did your first teachers teach you *how to read*? I doubt it. They taught you *how to master a skill*. Reading is what happened (or didn't happen) next, when you found what to do with the skill. Many cultures have a fable about babies in the womb possessing vast knowledge but losing it with the trauma of birth, and then having to go to school to re-learn what used to be there. The fable may or may not be true but in my own case I think I always read. I was brought up in a house where there were books everywhere. I was always a fast reader and still am; I skim-read fast to find out whether I want to go back and re-read and savour the material slowly. I can never be lonely, friendless, bored or in need of amusement if I have access to a library, a bookshelf or even just a solitary book. But since I have started to be rather personal in these remarks I have to admit that I don't read as much fiction as I used to. The sex and violence seem to be much more lurid and explicit these days—possibly because authors and publishers think this is the way to sell books—but I can't take too much of it. I can't make up my mind whether human beings have changed or I have.

61. Repentance

On the face of it, repentance is being sorry for a sin. I did wrong, I regret it, I will try and do better next time: "Let the wicked forsake his way and return to the Lord" (Isaiah Chapter 55). Most religions make this a major item on their agenda. Some say man is bound to sin, others that he is not necessarily a sinner but he does sin. The religious vocabulary is full of words like sin, temptation, guilt, confession, atonement, penance, pardon. It is good to recognise what you did wrong and to work through the guilt. However, when you analyse the word repentance you discover a broader concept—repentance as return to an earlier pristine reality. As a flower yearns for the sun, so everything in Creation yearns for perfection. The Kabbalah tradition attaches great importance to this notion. Whatever God created at the beginning of history was (see Genesis Chapters 1 and 2) "very good". The world, however, shattered to pieces like a glass that shatters when boiling water is poured into it. Man's task is to mend the world and restore the original perfection. This is possible on many levels, notably within the human being him- or herself: mend yourself, and you help to mend the world. This is repentance because the word derives from two Latin sources: "turn" and "again". Someone said, "Great is the art of writing music or literature. Greater still is the art of bringing about one's regeneration".

62. *Rules*

One can chafe under the burden of rules. "This is the way things are done here" is the rule about rules. It gives some people a comfort zone and others a straitjacket. There's a strong temptation to break loose and throw off all restraints. It's a blow for freedom, a sense of relief. You can go anywhere you choose, and do anything. Until you eventually hanker after a sense of structure in your life. The Indian writer Rabindranath Tagore points out that rules not only give you structure: they also—perhaps paradoxically—give you purpose, and release your potential.

"I have on my desk a violin string," he says. "It is not fixed into my violin. It is free to move in any direction. The only thing it is not free to do is to make music. Then I fix it into my violin. It is no longer free to move. But it is free for the first time to make music." When you learn a language you might well object to all the rules of grammar. "I want to speak!" you protest. You try speaking, in defiance of the laws of grammar. Maybe you make yourself clear, maybe you don't. Maybe all that happens is that people laugh at you. Then you try Tagore's advice and fix a metaphorical string into your linguistic violin. You are no longer free to use words as you will . . . but for the first time you can create intelligible sentences and even become eloquent.

63. *Sacrifice*

Ancient man took for granted that sacrifice was a way of worship. He used it to give utterance to his despair at being out of favour with the gods and to show his willingness to sacrifice things he loved and cherished, to prove his yearning for divine approval. The Hebrew Bible shears the sacrificial system of its excesses, toning them down and controlling the times, types and procedures of the sacrifice. Offerings were now mostly to show gratitude, to mark festive occasions, to seek the expiation of sins. The sacrifice was not a bribe to the Almighty but a symbol of a person's or community's need to articulate their wish to come close to God. Even when circumstances necessitated the suspension of sacrifices, the idea remained and became the touchstone of dedication to a belief, ideal or cause. Whether in science or culture, in following a faith or building a civilisation, nothing can be won without cost. Those who endure more and give more are the ones who live more and achieve more. This explains why so much religious ritual centres on the theme of the sacrifice of possessions, talents, time and sometimes even life itself. Serving a cause by means of sacrifice remains valid and valuable. The question is to which altar one's offering should be brought.

64. Silence

The zoo is a noisy place because of the animal sounds. This is the animals' way of making their presence felt and communicating. To most human beings these sounds are a mystery, though the Doctor Doolittle stories tried to solve it. All of Creation has its ways of communicating, though probably only humans have made speech into an art form. One of Martin Buber's great principles of dialogue is that silence is also a form of communication. People don't need to chatter all the time: companionable silence says a great deal. Biblical man already knew this when he heard that quietness and silence are means of addressing God: "Let all the earth be silent before Him" (Habakkuk Chapter 2), "To You silence is praise" (Psalm 65). When Aaron was in a state of shock he kept his peace (Numbers Chapter 16). There are times when you just have to speak, especially when keeping silent might let evil flourish unchecked. Those are times when you simply must say No to evil and Yes to good. But in many situations, refraining from speech can be the wisest thing. Not just because there is a saying, "Silence is the only successful substitute for brains", but because if someone else has said what was necessary you add nothing by piling up words. If you just have to express a feeling, opinion or reaction, you can do it by means of a gesture, a look, or even voting with your feet. If you really do have to speak you can still be economical with your words, saying enough but not indulging in verbal overkill.

65. *Sin*

Though sin is a rather awful thing, Hebrew has a series of wonderful words for it. One such word is *chet* (you pronounce the "*ch*" as in Loch Lomond). It really means to miss the mark. Presuming that every human being is fundamentally a good person trying to do the decent thing, a *chet* is when your good intentions go wrong. Another word is *averah*. Literally it's a transgression, but not necessarily against God. Rabbi Jack Riemer tells us that the storybook Jewish mother who believed so profoundly that chicken soup was the best thing ever invented, would serve you some soup and if you left part of it she would say, "Finish it. Otherwise it's an *averah*". Riemer comments, "This is about as good a definition of sin as you will find. For the real sins that most of us commit are not those of brutality or destruction, but sins of waste. If you don't become what you could potentially be, that's an *averah* . . . if you waste food, or time, or talent, or opportunities that God has given you, that's an *averah*. If you waste life, that is the greatest *averah* of all." A crime is to do something which hurts society. An *averah* is to do something which basically hurts yourself. Both are offences against God; the Bible has its lists of crimes against society, and also admonishes you (Deuteronomy Chapter 4), "Guard yourself carefully". Why would anyone commit an *averah* and be guilty of waste? Surely not out of wickedness: more probably out of stupidity.

66. *Song*

The birds flutter their wings and chirp out a song. The trees stand to attention and rustle their leaves. The dawn has a smile, and night has its eerie feel. Every part of nature somehow knows its task. Everything is singing to God in its own way. We humans unfortunately drown out their sound with our man-made cacophony. We should also be singing, but we're too busy shouting. We even shout when we purport to make music—we can no longer make soft sounds but have to turn the volume up to E—Excruciating. The next generation who say they like all this noise will probably suffer immense hearing impediments. A worse problem is that—unlike the birds and the trees—we have lost the ability to breathe in the fresh air and simply sing for joy at being alive. This sort of song does not require a concert-hall voice or a magnificent vocal range. You don't even need a voice at all—you can sing for joy without uttering a single sound.

67. *Sorrow*

Our mind knows that sorrow is inevitable, but when the sorrow comes it turns life upside down and inside out. Can it be prevented? Only if you never love, feel or care. In theory, that tough bracing yourself is possible, but in real life it never happens. As another part of this book says, the moment you say "Hello" you begin to say "Goodbye". The moment your life becomes knit with someone else's, you run the risk of the bond untying. When the tragedy occurs and you find yourself alone, you have to handle the moment somehow. Maybe you'll cry: maybe the tears won't come and you won't find release. Whether you weep now or later, the hole is still open and gaping. Well-meaning people will say, "You have to give yourself time. It's a great healer!" A platitude . . . not really true anyhow. It would be better if people held their tongues even when they are trying to help. The rent in one's heart will never be repaired; it won't go away. You'll have to work hard to hold onto the memory of the person you have lost. You'll often find yourself talking to them and asking what to do. Some day you'll meet again, but not in this life. You'll be tempted to be Queen Victoria and withdraw into yourself, but forget it. You have to move back into the world. The pain will still be in the background, but you'll be able to do normal things again, even to smile. In the meantime, enjoy your blessings whilst you have them.

68. *Study*

A person is revealed through what they do on the bus. Many people talk loudly into cell phones; others can't avoid listening in. Not that the conversations are really very interesting. Usually the person at the other end asks, "Where are you?" and the answer is, "On the bus!" One day the respondent might take the question philosophically and launch into an analysis of where they are in life. Other passengers engage in (generally inane) chats with the people around them. Some sit (or strap-hang) and watch the scenery or day-dream. A few—it used to be most—use the time to read. Once it was newspapers and books: now it's governed by the SMS and Kindle. All credit to those who can ignore what's happening around them and use the time for study. Study is the way to gain knowledge and to be stimulated to think. The bus is one place to study: a library or quiet room at home is even better. Through study you find things out; you walk the highways and byways of life. One is never too old to study. Elderly people used to be asked, "Why are you bothering at your age?"—and to answer, "I'm cramming for God's examinations!" A better answer would be, "To sharpen my mind, to understand the things that eluded me all my life, to be able to continue making an input into the world!"

69. Sunshine

Isaiah says (Chapter 49), "The Lord has forsaken me, the Lord has forgotten me!" The words resonate when things go wrong. When we cry, how can the sun still shine? When I was a teenager my mother died—the most devastating thing that had ever happened to me (Jeremiah Chapter 15 says, "Her sun went down while it was yet day"). On the way to the cemetery I couldn't understand why the whole world hadn't gone dark. I wanted to echo the Book of Joshua (Chapter 10), "Sun, stand thou still!" Yet no-one was saying that except me. I puzzled over the problem all my life until as a military chaplain I saw the war veterans going off for a beer the moment their city march had ended. With so many painful memories, how could the survivors push away the ghosts and make for a watering hole? Finally I realised: life has to go on. The sun still has to shine. The Bible says that the sun brings healing in its wings (Malachi Chapter 4). The sun makes things grow, it creates love and joy, it brings light and warmth (its solar energy has now begun to be harnessed for civilisation too). There might have been a night of darkness, but now there is a task for us to do. The sun invites us to pursue the task. Zangwill praises someone in these words, "A sunbeam took human shape when he was born". When we accept the healing hand of the sun we create sunbeams that allow us to smile and the world to feel better.

70. *Superstition*

Laugh at it as much as you like—black cats, walking under ladders and the rest—but let's say something good about superstition. Popular beliefs and usages—even popular neuroses—have their place. They are an expression of democracy; they give respect to what the people say. True, they are generally primitive and non-rational, but they have their role in the development of society and civilisation. They give people stable customs and respect for tradition. They often originated in actual events—a person who walked under a ladder got hurt when the ladder collapsed; someone who saw a black cat had a run of bad luck. What's wrong with superstitions is their basis—fear "You're different: therefore—though I wouldn't say it publicly—I'm scared of you!"), imagination ("I think there's something strange about you: therefore you don't fit in!"), enslavement of the mind ("Everyone says people like you are a danger!"), intolerance based on accidents of birth ("You were born black: therefore you're unintelligent!" "You were born a woman: therefore you're a witch!" "You were born a Jew: therefore you're tight-fisted!"). Biblical teaching is adamantly opposed to magic and necromancy (look at Leviticus 19) It also stands for the dignity of every human being, even if they're a bit different—all are made in the image of God (look at the beginning of Genesis), and if you don't like what they are, go and complain to the Creator. But be warned. He might take their side and not yours.

71. *Talk*

Once upon a time people used to say, "Sticks and stones will break your bones, but names will never hurt you". The pity is that it isn't true. Name-calling *does* hurt you: it wounds your feelings, it disturbs the climate of society, it generally leads to worse things. Talking can make the world better—and it can also make it much more evil. Solomon Ibn Gavirol said, "If I utter a word, it becomes my master . . . but if

I don't utter it, I remain its master". The ability to talk is a precious gift; we should be careful how we use it. Two ancient kings, David and Solomon, father and son, each said something memorable about talk. David said (Psalm 34), "Guard your tongue from evil and your lips from speaking guile"; Solomon said (Proverbs 18), "Death and life are in the power of the tongue". So here are Ten Commandments of Talk:

1. Talk little, and keep it short.
2. Talk only when your words will be useful.
3. Talk kindly, not with barbs that wound.
4. Talk decency, not coarse dirt.
5. Talk the truth, but say it nicely.
6. Talk honestly, not just what the other person expects you to say.
7. Think before you talk.
8. Make your point and then hold your tongue.
9. Talk less and do more: talk won't feed the hungry.
10. Dare to stand out and speak out whenever you see evil.

72. Time

Isaac Watts' famous hymn based on Psalm 90 says, "Time, like an ever-rolling stream, bears all its sons away; they fly forgotten, as a dream dies at the opening day". Beautiful words, but too morbid by far. Think of all the popular phrases involving the word "time"—tell the time, mark time, time after time, time's up, and the public-house refrain, "Time, gentlemen, please" . . . Time signifies movement. Nothing stands still. Yes, there comes a moment when your time's up and the stream bears you away—but in the meantime (another useful "time" word) every day should be a boon with its own blessing. No moment should be wasted or rushed through. The world is constantly on the move. There is a recurring time pattern everywhere: birth, growth, development, death. Time is not only the way of measuring the movement. It is the God-given opening of opportunities. Here is something that Albert Einstein wrote: "A hundred times every day I remind myself that my inner and outer life depend on the labours of other men, living and dead, and that I must exert myself in order to give in the measure as

I have received". A hundred (or more) times a day we each have the opportunity to do something for other people—and for ourselves.

73. *Tolerance*

"I tolerate you." Of course I do. It sounds good, but it's too patronising. What does it mean? I suffer your presence. I endure you. So look what a martyr I am! I'd rather you weren't there, but I put up with you! If that's tolerance, then tolerance is all right as far as it goes—but it doesn't go far enough. Better than mere tolerance is the ability to celebrate one another, to say, "God made me—and He made you too! God has room for you in His world—and I have room for you in my world!" We're not all the same, and there's no reason why we should be. We each have our own mixture of heredity and environment, our own commitments and conscience, our own views and values. J.B. Soloveitchik said that man and woman will never entirely understand one another, but they can still love each other. You and I will never be able to get inside each other's head and understand our respective ways of thinking and being, but we can appreciate and celebrate each other. The Kotzker Rebbe said, "I am I—because you are you". Call it tolerance if you wish. I prefer the phrase *good will*—that is, unless you can find a better description.

74. *Travel*

For Cain, the first person ever to be born on earth, travel was nothing but a curse. He killed his brother Abel and was sentenced to roam the world for ever. It was bound to be an eerie, lonesome experience. The beauties of Nature were there, but there was no populace, no culture, to encounter or interact with, not even anyone to complain about. What about modern-day travel? Travel these days is also no great pleasure, not because there are no interesting people around but because they give us such problems. We know what it is to sit next to the passenger from hell, to be pointedly ignored by the indifferent cabin attendant, browbeaten by the petty tyrant at the security desk, talked at by the gramophone-record tour guide, charged through the nose by everyone and for everything, and bamboozled by the illogical complex of air flights and fares. How absurdly grateful we are when occasionally an airport or hotel check-in desk says we're being upgraded. In the end we get home and decide that isn't such a bad place after all. We resolve not to budge again but to limit our travel to vicarious roaming by means of the computer, television and personal imagination. But then our resolve fails and we book the next trip, assuring ourselves that it has to be better this time.

75. Trees

It sounds like heavy sarcasm when the Bible declares that in wartime an army should not attack the trees—"Is the tree of the field a man that you should attack it?"(Deuteronomy Chapter 20). The question implies, "What has the tree ever done to you that you should assail it?" Fair enough, but why should you attack a human being either? What have the ordinary human beings on the opposing side ever done to you that you should want to harm them? There was a Christmas truce between German and allied troops in World War I. For a day both sides laid down their arms and celebrated Christmas by fraternising and showing each other photos of their families. When the day was over, however, it was business as usual; the guns started firing and each side killed the other. Crazy. From the ethical point of view, people and trees should be treated alike. "Save the trees" is fair enough, but so is "Save the human beings". But when you attack either of them, there is a difference. Human beings can (at least sometimes) escape and survive, whilst the trees are fixtures. They have no chance of running away and are doomed the moment you target them. Add the other reasons for protecting the trees—their shade, their fruit, their beauty, their reinforcement of the soil. Please be good to them.

76. Truth

There is truth—and there are truths. Night follows day—that's a truth. One and one are two—that's a truth. The question is why truths are true. One answer is to call them axioms which are self-evident and fixed in the structure of the world. Another approach is historical—"These things have been proved so often in the past that now we rely on being heirs to accepted fact". A third approach is the religious one—"Two and two, *with the help of God*, make four." All three approaches have become difficult in an age in which everything nailed down is coming loose, nothing is taken for granted, history is rewritten, and religion is cast aside. It looks as though we are going to have to start from square one again and re-establish the basis of truth on the foundation of our own investigation. What makes the task more complicated is that hardly anyone has an objective mind any more. Almost everyone is under the influence of prejudice, persuasion and politics. People and nations tell lies without compunction and the media peddle half-truths without conscience. It is hard to live at such a time, hard to maintain constant vigilance to expose the falsehoods and argue for the facts. The honest religious believer, however, finds comfort in the assurance that truth is the seal of the Almighty and in the end nothing can withstand it.

77. Wisdom

A fable tells that a king told his closest counsellor, "Ask what you will, and it will be granted thee". The counsellor asked for the hand of the king's only daughter in marriage, knowing that in that way everything else would become his. Similarly God asked King Solomon what his greatest wish was (I Kings Chapter 3), and the answer was "Wisdom!" In his book *Students, Scholars and Saints*, Louis Ginzberg asked himself what made a person into a sage. A tenacious memory? Quick perception? Other ways of using the mind? All these, he concluded, had to be in place, but the crucial element was "to be in possession of a great soul". Wisdom engages both mind and soul. How does it operate? It sums up a situation, recognises the central issue, and knows what to do and how to do it. In the Bible, Jethro, the father-in-law of Moses, had that gift. Moses was the leader, the teacher, the inspirer, the prophet—but Jethro provided the practical guidance that saved Moses from becoming burnt out and disappearing from history. There's a lot of truth in the proverb, "Better a slap from the wise than a kiss from a fool".

78. Work

Western society is based, at least theoretically, on the Ten Commandments. Concerning work the Decalogue says, "Work six days and keep the seventh as a Sabbath". Human beings need both activity and rest. Problem: rest is regarded as a foretaste of heaven. But so, at least in the Jewish tradition, is work. Judaism says the righteous are still active and busy in the next world, doing good deeds and getting closer to God. On earth there's maybe no rest for the wicked, and it's no blessing to have them constantly scheming and sinning. In heaven there's nothing for the wicked to do—but they won't be there anyhow. In heaven, and on earth too in the messianic Utopia, many professions will be redundant. Criminality certainly: warfare too, even medicine (because there will be no disease), even the law (since there'll be no disputes). But in the meantime the Book of Ecclesiastes has the right idea—"Whatever your hand finds to do, do it with all your might" (Chapter 9). It's not only might and energy you should bring to your task, but honesty, care, and pride in your work. What you get paid is not the main thing, though the pay and the working conditions have to be fair, but it is your attitude and work ethic that matter most. Even if it's voluntary work you're doing, that also needs a work ethic and a good attitude.

79. Worry

There's a new way of answering the question, "How's things?" "How's things? No worries!" In some places there's an alternative answer, "She's apples!" I thought this was a compliment to me, bearing in mind my surname, but I fear I was wrong. In religious circles they say, "How's things? Thank God!" It's nice and pious to say, "Thank God!", but the answer possibly needs more substance. "No worries!" doesn't help much, because if someone really lacks worries that would be something to worry about. What does *worry* mean? "Things aren't going well, in the big wide world or in my own microcosm"? "I'm not sure I'll be able to cope"? There are grounds for worry in what others are (or aren't) doing, and in our own effectiveness. We probably also worry about how God is running His universe: there are times when He really needs our support. The likelihood is that He will say, "That's why I created you, to be My partners, to give Me a hand". On the whole, I suppose we worry more about the world than about the Creator. From the moral standpoint it's not the best of all possible worlds. Things could be better, and we can help to make them so. It's a daunting responsibility, and we should be worrying about how to get there.

80. *Youth*

Youth is wasted on the young. That's the consensus of the older generation, echoing the words of George Bernard Shaw. Older people are jealous of the energy, the freshness, the resilience, the idealism of the young. A bit the worse for wear, older people wonder where their strength and optimism have gone, and they find an answer: the young people have robbed the cupboard and left the oldies physically and psychologically threadbare. The accusation isn't quite fair. The young don't have it so easy; the old are not as poorly off as they claim. To illustrate let me recall a sermon I once gave. My theme was, "The Greatest Day of My Life". I examined yesterday, today and tomorrow, and argued that they all had their good points. My conclusion was that the best day of my life was potentially *every day*. If we take control of our lives, every day can be a great day. For that you don't have to be young, though it helps. It also doesn't hurt to be old or on the way to it. It's all a question of attitude. One of the big differences is that on the whole the young lack responsibilities and the old are weighed down by them. You can't change that, but you can still choose to make a given day into a great one. It's good to be young. Enjoy it. However . . . being old can also turn out to be quite bearable.

About The Author

Raymond Apple is a rabbi. For many years he was spiritual head of the Great Synagogue in Sydney and a leading figure in Australian public life. He is passionately concerned for the quality of society and amongst other compliments has been called "the great communicator" and "the rabbi of tolerance". His interests range from A to Z—from Aboriginal Reconciliation to Zionism—with many things in between such as law, history and education. This book dips into his thoughts on people and their problems.